The Ultimate Pasta Cookbook

A Variety of Delicious Pasta Recipes to Try Out!

BY: Valeria Ray

License Notes

Copyright © 2020 Valeria Ray All Rights Reserved

All rights to the content of this book are reserved by the Author without exception unless permission is given stating otherwise.

The Author have no claims as to the authenticity of the content and the Reader bears all responsibility and risk when following the content. The Author is not liable for any reparations, damages, accidents, injuries or other incidents occurring from the Reader following all or part of this publication.

Table of Contents

Introduction 6

    Cajun Chicken Pastas 7

    Pesto Cavatappi From Noodles & Company 10

    Skipping Rattlesnake Pasta 12

    Kung Pao Spaghetti 15

    3 Cheeses Chicken Penne 18

    Mac N' Cheese 21

    Green Tomato Pasta 23

    Pilli Pilli Pasta Sauce 25

    Pasta Milano 27

    Lobster Ravioli 29

    Lemon Chicken with Angel Hair Pasta 31

    Baked Penne Casserole with Leeks and Green Peas 34

    Lobster Fra Diavolo 37

    Spaghetti with Anchovies - Spaghetti con Acciughe 40

Spaghetti with Garlic Sauce 42

Authentic homemade pasta sauce recipe 44

Mostaccioli and Pork Meatballs 46

Manicotti with Cheese Filling 49

Squash Ravioli - Tortei de Moranga 51

Bucatini with Quail Sauce 55

Lemony basil orzo pasta salad 58

Spaghetti with Meatballs 60

Mexican Mac and Cheese 63

Pasta Pizza Chicken Casserole 66

Arrabiata Sauce 68

Cheese and Salsa Chicken Casserole 70

Lasagna 72

Linguine with Tuna Puttanesca 74

Spicy Pasta Alfredo Casserole 77

Tortellini Chicken Primavera 79

Conclusion 81

About the Author 82

Author's Afterthoughts 83

Introduction

Looking for new pasta recipes that you can make at home? If your answer is yes, this book is for you! From casseroles to soups and salads, there are a ton of delicious pasta recipes here that you whip up easily and everyone will love!

All the recipes in this recipe book are easy and can be made by almost everyone! Plus, the recipes are detailed with step-by-step instructions and can be easily doubled or tripled, depending on the occasion. So, choose a recipe and let's get started!

Cajun Chicken Pastas

Perfectly spiced and absolutely delicious!

Servings: 4

Time: 20 minutes

Ingredient

- 2 chicken breasts, boneless and skinles
- ½ tbsp. salt
- 1 tbsp. olive oil, divided
- 3 quarts water
- 2 tbsp. unsalted butter
- 3 garlic cloves, minced
- 1 cup heavy cream
- 8 ounces penne pasta
- ½ tsp lemon zest
- ¼ cup Parmesan cheese, shredded
- Salt and black pepper, to taste
- 1 tbsp. oil
- 1 tbsp. Cajun seasoning
- 2 Roma tomatoes, diced
- 2 tbsp. parsley chopped

Directions

Place chicken in a Ziploc bag. Add 1 tbsp. oil and Cajun seasoning. Using your hands, combine chicken and mixture until well-coated. Seal tightly and set aside to marinate.

Cook pasta in a pot filled with salt and boiling water. Follow package instructions. Drain and set aside.

In a skillet, heat butter over med heat. Sauté garlic for 1 minute or until aromatic. Slowly add cream, followed by lemon zest. Cook for 1 minute, stirring continuously until fully blended. Toss in Parmesan cheese. Mix until sauce is a little thick, then add salt and pepper. Add pasta and combine until well-coated. Transfer onto a bowl and keep warm.

In a separate skillet, heat remaining oil. Cook chicken over med-high heat for about 5 minutes on each side or until fully cooked through. Transfer onto chopping board and cut into thin strips.

Top pasta with chicken and sprinkle with tomatoes and parsley on top.

Serve.

Pesto Cavatappi From Noodles & Company

Easy, elegant, and yummy!

Servings: 8

Time: 20 minutes

Ingredient

- 4 quarts water
- 1 tbsp. salt
- 1-pound macaroni pasta
- 1 tsp olive oil
- 1 cup grated Parmesan cheese
- ¼ cup chicken broth
- a large tomato, finely chopped
- 4-ounce mushrooms, finely chopped
- ¼ cup dry white wine
- ¼ cup heavy cream
- 1 cup pesto

Instructions:

Add water and salt to a pot. Bring to a boil. Put in pasta and then cook for 10 minutes or until al dente. Drain and set aside.

In a pan, heat oil. Sauté tomatoes and mushrooms for 5 minutes. Pour in broth, wine, and cream. Bring to a boil. Reduce heat to med and simmer for 2 minutes or until mixture is thick. Stir in pesto and cook for another 2 minutes. Toss in pasta. Mix until fully coated.

Transfer onto plates and sprinkle with Parmesan cheese.

Skipping Rattlesnake Pasta

This delicious pasta recipe combines 2 favorite kinds of cheeses!

Servings: 6

Time: 25 minutes

Ingredient

Pasta:

- 4 quart
- 1-pound penne pasta
- 1 dash of salt
- Chicken:
- 2 tbsp. butter
- 2 cloves garlic, finely chopped
- ½ tbsp. Italian seasoning
- 1-pound chicken breast, boneless and skinless, cut into small square

Sauce:

- 4 tbsp. butter
- 2 cloves garlic, finely chopped
- ¼ cup all-purpose flour
- 1 tbsp. salt
- ¾ tsp white pepper
- 2 cups milk
- 1 cup half-and-half
- ¾ cup Parmesan cheese, shredded
- 8 ounces Colby cheese, shredded
- 3 jalapeno peppers, chopped

Direction

In a pot of boiling water, add salt, and cook pasta according to package instructions. Drain well and set aside.

To prepare the chicken, heat butter in a pan. Sauté garlic and Italian seasoning for 1 minute. Add chicken and cook 5-7 minutes or until cooked thoroughly, flipping halfway through. Transfer onto a plate once. Set aside.

In the same pan, prepare the sauce. Add butter and heat until melted. Stir in garlic and continue cooking 30 seconds. Then, add flour, salt, and pepper. Cook for 2 more minutes, stirring continuously. Pour in milk and half-and-half. Keep stirring until sauce turns thick and smooth.

Toss in chicken, jalapeno peppers, and pasta. Stir until combined.

Serve.

Kung Pao Spaghetti

This recipe is a guaranteed crowd pleaser!

Servings: 4

Time: 20 minutes

Ingredient

- 1-pound spaghetti
- 2 tbsp. vegetable oil
- 3 chicken breasts, boneless and skinles
- Salt and pepper, to taste
- 4 garlic cloves, finely chopped
- ½ cup dry roasted peanut
- 6 green onions, cut into half-inch piece
- 10-12 Dried bird eyes hot pepper

Sauce:

- ½ cup soy sauce
- ½ cup chicken broth
- ½ cup dry sherry
- 2 tbsp. red chili paste with garlic
- ¼ cup sugar
- 2 tbsp. red wine vinegar
- 2 tbsp. cornstarch
- 1 tbsp. sesame oil

Directions

Follow instructions on package to cook spaghetti noodles. Drain and set aside.

Add oil to a large pan over med-high heat. Generously season chicken, then add to pan once hot. Cook for about 3 to 4 minutes. Turn chicken over and cook for another 3 to 4 minutes. Remove from heat and allow to cool.

Combine all sauce ingredients in a bowl.

Once chicken has cooled, chop chicken into small pieces. Set aside.

Return pan to heat. Add garlic and sauté for about 1 minute until aromatic. Pour in prepared sauce, then stir. Set to boil then lower heat and simmer for about 1 to 2 minutes or until liquid thickens. Add pasta, cooked chicken, peanuts, hot peppers, and scallions. Mix well.

Serve.

3 Cheeses Chicken Penne

This Applebee dish is an old timer favorite!

Servings: 4

Time: 1 hour

Ingredient

- 2 boneless skinless chicken breast
- 15 ounces Alfredo sauce
- 1 cup Italian salad dressing
- 6 tbsp. olive oil, divided
- 8 ounces combination mozzarella, Parmesan, and provolone cheeses, grated
- 4 roma tomatoes, seeded and diced
- 3 cups penne pasta
- 4 tbsp. fresh basil, diced
- 2 cloves garlic, finely chopped
- Shredded parmesan cheese for serving

Directions

Preheat oven to 350°F.

In a bowl, add chicken then drizzle with Italian dressing. Mix to fully coat chicken with dressing. Cover using plastic wrap and keep inside refrigerator overnight but, if you're in a hurry, at least 2 hours is fine.

Follow instructions on package to cook penne pasta. Drain, then set aside.

Brush 3 tbsp. oil onto grates of grill then preheat to med-high heat. Add marinated chicken onto grill, discarding the marinade. Cook chicken until both sides are fully cooked and internal temperature measures 165°F. Remove from grill. Set aside until cool enough to handle. Then, cut chicken into thin slices.

In a large bowl, add cooked noodles, Alfredo sauce, and grilled chicken. Mix until combined.

Drizzle remaining oil onto large casserole pan, then pour noodle mixture inside. Sprinkle cheeses on top. Bake for 15-20 minutes until cheese turns a golden and edges of mixture begins to bubble. Remove from oven.

Mix tomatoes, basil, and garlic in a bowl. Add on top of pasta.

Sprinkle parmesan cheese before serving.

Mac N' Cheese

A quick and easy mac n cheese that is guaranteed to be a hit!

Servings: 6

Time: 20 minutes

Ingredient

- 1 8-ounce package spiral pasta
- 2 tbsp. butter
- 2 tbsp. all-purpose flour
- 1 ¾ cups whole milk
- 1 ¼ cups diced processed cheese like Velveeta™
- ¼ tsp dry mustard
- ½ tsp onion powder
- 1 tsp salt
- Pepper, to taste

Directions

Cook pasta according to package instructions. Drain, then set aside.

To prepare sauce make the roux with four and butter over med-low heat in a large deep skillet. Add milk and whisk until well blended. Add cheese, mustard, salt, and pepper. Keep stirring until smooth.

Once pasta is cooked, transfer to a serving bowl. Pour cheese mixture on top. Toss to combine.

Serve warm.

Green Tomato Pasta

Delicious spaghetti recipe with garlic and green tomatoes.

Makes: 4 servings

Prep: 10 mins

Cook: 20 mins

Ingredient

- 4 cups spaghetti
- 4 large green tomatoes, thinly sliced (1/8-inch thick)
- Salt and pepper, to taste
- 1 cup flour
- Vegetable oil, for frying
- 2 garlic cloves, minced
- 1/4 cup parmesan cheese, grated

Directions

Prepare spaghetti according to directions; & drain well and set aside.

Season tomatoes with salt and pepper. Coat with flour & fry in hot oil with garlic until golden brown. Do not overcook. Place fried tomato slices on top of hot, cooked pasta. Top with parmesan cheese and serve immediately.

Pilli Pilli Pasta Sauce

This is a simple tomato based hot sauce that is great with pasta or as a relish with sandwiches.

Cooking Time: 10 minutes

Makes: One 16 oz.

List of Ingredient

- Tomato Sauce (2 cups)
- Lemon Juice (½ cup)
- Onions (½ cup, minced)
- Garlic Powder (1 tbsp.)
- Red Crushed Pepper (1 tbsp.)

Methods:

Put all ingredients into a two-quart bowl and blend to combine. Cover the container and refrigerate.

Enjoy with seafood or use as a relish.

Pasta Milano

Another pasta favorite from Macaroni Grill!

Servings: 6

Time: 20 minutes

Ingredient

- 1-pound bowtie pasta
- 2 tsp olive oil
- 1-pound chicken, chopped into small piece
- 1 12-ounce package mushrooms, chopped
- 1 cup onion, minced
- 2 garlic cloves, finely minced
- ½ cup sun dried tomatoes, diced
- 1½ cups half and half
- 1 tbsp. butter, softened
- ½ cup Parmesan cheese, shredded, plus some more for serving
- 1 tsp black pepper, ground
- 1 tbsp. fresh basil, minced

Directions

Follow instructions on package to cook bowtie pasta. Drain, then set aside.

Add oil to a pan over med-high heat. Once hot, add chicken and stir-fry for about 5 to 6 minutes until cooked through. Set chicken aside onto a plate.

In the same pan, toss in mushrooms, onions, garlic, and sun-dried tomatoes. Sauté until onions turn soft and mushrooms become a light brown, then sprinkle salt and pepper to season. Return chicken to pan and mix.

Mix half and half, butter, Parmesan, pepper, and basil in a small bowl.

Add half and half mixture to pan. Stir, and let simmer for about 3 to 4 minutes or until pan ingredients are thoroughly heated. Mix in pasta until coated well.

Serve.

Lobster Ravioli

Is there anything more decadent than seafood and pasta? Enjoy this dish with friends who are sure to be impressed by your lobster endeavor.

Serves 10

Total Time: 30mins

Ingredient

- 2 pounds fresh uncooked lobster meat
- 2 bunches leeks
- 1/2 bunch fresh parsley
- Fresh-cracked black pepper
- 1 recipe classic pasta dough, uncut and uncooked

Directions

Roughly chop lobster meat into bite-sized pieces. Thoroughly wash and dry the leeks. Thinly slice. Clean and chop the parsley.

In a large bowl, combine lobster, leeks, parsley, and black pepper.

Roll out pasta onto a floured surface into sheets about 1/2 inch thick. Cut into circles 3 inches in diameter.

Spoon teaspoonfuls of the lobster mixture onto the centers of the circles. Lightly paint the outer edge of the pasta with a tiny amount of water, fold in half, and seal by pressing closed with your fingers.

Bring 2 gallons of water to a slow boil. Then add in ravioli and cook until al dente, approximately 10 minutes.

Serve the ravioli with the sauce of your choice and sprinkle with black pepper.

Lemon Chicken with Angel Hair Pasta

The low carb noodles make this perfect for keto!

Time: 30m

Servings: 3

Nutritional Facts Per serving:

- Protein Counts: 39 g
- Total Fats: 16 g
- Calories: 325
- Net Carbohydrates: 2 g

Ingredient

- Chicken breast (1 lb./454 g)
- Large lemon (1)
- Shirataki angel hair noodles (2, 7-oz./200 g pkg.)
- Garlic (1 large clove)
- XCT oil/another cooking oil (1 tbsp.)
- Organic garlic (1 large clove)
- Dried oregano (.5 tsp.) or Minced fresh oregano - leaves only (1 tsp.)
- Himalayan pink salt (.5 tsp.)
- Butter or ghee (2 tbsp.)
- Collagelatin/another grass-fed gelatin (1 tbsp.)
- Fresh oregano - leaves only (1-2 tbsp.)

Directions

Squeeze the juice and zest from the lemon into separate containers.

Prepare the noodles, and rinse for 15 seconds. Boil for two minutes in a saucepan of boiling water. Drain the noodles and arrange them in a dry skillet using the medium temperature heat setting. "Dry roast" them for one minute. Cool them in the pan for two to three minutes.

Using the med-high temperature setting, warm a cast-iron skillet with oil.

Mince the chicken into small pieces and toss into the skillet with the minced garlic, salt, and dried oregano.

Sauté until thoroughly cooked for about eight to ten minutes. Stir occasionally. Transfer the chicken into a mixing bowl and set it aside.

Lower the pan temperature setting to medium. Pour in the lemon juice to deglaze the pan. Add butter and whisk in the gelatin to finish.

Mix the noodles and chicken back into the skillet, tossing thoroughly to combine.

Serve topped with lemon zest and a garnish of fresh oregano.

Baked Penne Casserole with Leeks and Green Peas

A delicious pasta casserole with leeks, peas, bell peppers, and eggs.

Makes: 4 servings

Prep: 25 mins

Cook: 20 mins

Ingredient

- Butter for greasing the baking pan
- ½ cup extra virgin olive oil
- 2 tablespoons finely chopped fresh Italian parsley
- 2 leeks, cleaned and chopped (white part only)
- 1 red bell pepper, cored, seeded, & diced
- ¾ pound penne
- 4 large eggs
- 6 ounces fresh or frozen green peas Salt and freshly ground black pepper
- ¼ cup milk
- 1/3 cup (about 1 ounce) freshly grated Parmesan cheese, plus more for passing at the table

Directions

Preheat oven to 350°F & then grease an 8-x-8-inch baking pan with butter

Warm the oil in a large frying pan overheat. Add the leeks and the red pepper and sauté until they begin to soften, 3-4 min. Add the green peas and a few tablespoons of hot water and cook for another 15 minutes, or until the peas are tender. Season with salt and pepper to taste.

Bring water to boil on high heat. Add in a small fistful of salt and the penne and boil until the penne is tender. Save 1 cup of the water & drain the pasta in a colander. Add the pasta to the condimento in the frying pan and place over high heat. Stir them together and sauté for 1 minute, adding pasta water to make the pasta wet and slippery. Add the parsley and mix again. Turn off the heat and let the pasta cool to room temperature.

While the pasta is cooling, beat the eggs with the Parmesan cheese, milk, and salt and pepper to taste. Add the eggs to the cooled pasta and stir to mix them together. Spoon the pasta into the prepared baking pan. Press down lightly on the pasta to make it even. Place the pan in the oven and bake for 20 minutes, or until the crust is light golden brown. Remove & let the pasta rest for a few minutes. Turn it out onto a serving dish & serve immediately with freshly grated Parmesan on the table.

Lobster Fra Diavolo

When you want to make an impression, serve this opulent lobster pasta dish. Fra Diavolo translates as devil-monk, which is the name given to spicy sauce for seafood or pasta. This dish is mostly reserved for special occasions and a holiday feast.

Portions: 4-6

Total Time: 1hour 5mins

Ingredient

- 3 tbsp. virgin olive oil
- 2 garlic cloves (finely chopped)
- 1 medium onion (peeled, finely chopped)
- 1 cup Italian dry white wine
- 3 cups chopped, canned Italian tomato
- 2 tbsp. fresh basil (finely chopped)
- Red pepper flakes
- 2 (1½ pound) lobsters
- 1-pound fresh linguine
- 3 tbsp. finely chopped parsley

Directions

In a large saucepan, heat the oil.

Add onions to pan and cook till onions turn translucent and softened, next add the chopped garlic.

Cook the garlic for 60-90 seconds, or until it emits its fragrance.

Add the dry white wine and cook until the liquid reduces by half.

Next, add the canned tomatoes and stir to combine.

Season according to taste. Sprinkle in the fresh basil and add a dash of red pepper flakes.

Cook for 12-15 minutes over a low heat.

Cut each of the lobster in half, across their length, and add to the sauce.

Cook for 15-20 minutes on low, until bright pink and the lobster meat is sufficiently cooked.

Remove the lobster from the sauce and cut the lobster meat from the claws and the tail and cut into bite-sized pieces.

Return the lobster meat to the sauce and keep warm.

In the meantime, and while the lobster is cooking, add salted water to a pot and bring to boil.

Add pasta and cook al dente.

Drain return it to the pot.

Add 2-3 ladles of sauce to the linguine and over moderate heat, stir well to combine.

Evenly divide the linguine into 4 pasta bowls and top with the remaining sauce.

Sprinkle parsley over the top and serve.

Spaghetti with Anchovies - Spaghetti con Acciughe

This particular recipe features as one of the seven dishes served on Christmas Eve. Each region of Italy has its own typical dishes; cod fritters in Naples, Pasta, broccoli, and arzilla fish soup in Rome and spaghetti with anchovies in Calabria.

Portions: 8

Total Time: 30mins

Ingredient

- 1 pound pasta
- 3 tbsp. extra virgin olive oil
- 2 large cloves garlic (chopped)
- 14 ounces anchovy fillets (chopped)
- ½ tsp crushed red pepper flakes
- 4 tbsp. dried breadcrumbs

Directions

Cook the pasta according to manufacturer instructions in salted boiling water.

a frying pan over moderate heat, heat the olive oil and add the garlic, cooking until it emits its fragrance and begins to brown.

Remove the pieces of garlic from the pan and add the anchovies. Mash the anchovies, using a wooden spoon, until they dissolve in the oil. Add the crushed red pepper and reduce the heat, cooking for 2-3 minutes.

Drain the pasta and top with anchovy sauce.

Drizzle with olive oil and scatter with breadcrumbs.

Spaghetti with Garlic Sauce

A simple, 5-ingredient recipe with garlic, parsley, and butter.

Makes: 4 servings

Prep: 10 mins

Cook: 10 mins

Ingredient

- 1 lb. spaghetti, cooked
- 1/2 cup butter
- 1/2 cup extra-virgin olive oil
- 4 small cloves garlic, minced
- 2 tablespoons fresh parsley, chopped
- Parmesan cheese, grated

Directions

Cook pasta according to directions; drain & set aside.

Meanwhile, melt butter in a large pan. Add olive oil. Sauté minced garlic in oil until golden brown. Add cooked spaghetti and parsley. Cook over low heat until heated through. Serve with grated Parmesan cheese.

Authentic homemade pasta sauce recipe

This delicious pasta sauce is authentic and easy to prep!

Time: 2hr

Serving Size: 1 pint

Ingredient

- 1 medium onion, finely chopped
- 2 tablespoons olive oil
- 500 grams can whole/chopped Italian plum tomatoes
- 2 teaspoons concentrated tomato puree
- 1 tablespoon white wine vinegar
- 3 teaspoons sugar

Directions:

In a large saucepan, gently sauté the onion in the oil until transparent. Add the tomato and bring to the boil. Once simmering, add the tomato puree, the vinegar and sugar. Simmer for a full hour, using a wooden spoon to break up any tomato pieces. If the sauce still has pieces of tomato, pass through a sieve before bottling and storing in the refrigerator for up to two weeks. Use as a base for more complex meat sauces for pasta.

Mostaccioli and Pork Meatballs

Delicious meatball recipe with sausage, garlic, and tomatoes.

Makes: 8 servings

Prep: 10 mins

Cook: 2 hrs. 40 mins

Ingredient

Sauce:

- 1 to 2 lbs. mild sausage (may substitute 1/2 hot and 1/2 sweet sausage)
- 1 tbsp. parsley
- 1 tbsp. oregano
- 1/8 tsp. basil
- 6 large cloves garlic, minced
- 1 tsp. salt
- 3 (29 oz.) cans tomato puree
- 3 (6 oz. can) tomato paste
- 1 onion, whole

Meatballs:

- 1.5 to 3 lb. ground pork
- 2 eggs, beaten
- 1 (1.5 oz.) package meat loaf seasoning mix
- 1 clove garlic, finely chopped
- 1 tbsp. parsley
- Salt and pepper, to taste
- 4 slices bread
- 1/2 cup milk
- 3/4 cup breadcrumbs
- 1/4 cup Parmesan cheese, grated

Pasta:

- 1 to 2 lbs. mostaccioli

Directions

Cook the pasta; drain and set aside.

Sauce: Brown sausage in large pot. Cook, covered, for 30 minutes. Remove sausage, leaving most of the fat for flavor. Add garlic, basil, oregano, parsley, and salt; stir. Add tomato puree and tomato paste; mix well. Fill both tomato puree and paste cans with water and add to sauce; mix well. Add whole onion (remove just before serving). Simmer at least 2 hours.

Meatballs: In a bowl, mix eggs, parsley, ground pork, garlic, seasoning mix, salt and pepper. In a bowl, soak slices of bread in milk.

Squeeze out excess milk and break bread apart into small pieces. Combine bread, bread crumbs and Parmesan cheese. Add to ground pork and mix thoroughly. Shape into balls & bake at 350 degrees F. for 40 minutes. Add to sauce and serve over pasta.

Pasta: Prepare pasta according to package directions. Drain and rinse well with hot water. Return pasta to pan and stir in a small amount of sauce to prevent sticking. When serving, top with sauce.

Manicotti with Cheese Filling

Manicotti are pasta tubes that are stuffed and then baked. In this recipe, we're filling them with a delicious 3-cheese mixture.

Makes: 8 servings

Prep: 10 mins

Cook: 55 mins

Ingredient

- 1 (8 oz.) package manicotti
- 2 cups mozzarella cheese, shredded
- 2 cups (15 oz.) ricotta cheese
- 1/4 cup Parmesan cheese, grated
- 2 tablespoons parsley, chopped
- 1/2 teaspoon salt
- 1/4 teaspoon pepper
- 1 (32 oz.) jar spaghetti sauce

Directions

Cook pasta according to directions; drain & set aside. Cool in a single layer on parchment paper, aluminum foil or baking sheets to prevent manicotti from sticking together.

In a bowl, mix mozzarella cheese, parsley, ricotta cheese, Parmesan cheese, salt and pepper. Spoon cheese filling mixture into manicotti. Spread a thin layer of the jar sauce on bottom of a 13x9-inch pan. Arrange the pasta in a layer on top of sauce. Top with remaining sauce. Cover dish with aluminum foil. Bake at 350F. for 40 mins. Remove foil; bake 15 mins longer.

Squash Ravioli - Tortei de Moranga

If you go to the Serrana region of Rio Grande do Sul, you will find many restaurants called galeteria serving tortei de moranga, a delicious squash-filled ravioli that is largely cherished in that region.

Ingredient

- Serves 4 to 6

For the filling:

- 4 tablespoons (1/2 stick/60 g) unsalted butter
- 12 ounces (340 g) ripe kabocha squash, peeled, seeded, and cut into 1/2 in (13 mm) cubes
- 2 tablespoons (11 g) grated Parmesan
- 1 teaspoon freshly ground nutmeg
- Salt and freshly ground white pepper

For the dough:

- 3 cups (360 g) all-purpose flour
- 5 large eggs, beaten
- 1 tablespoon kosher salt
- 2 tablespoons (30 ml) olive oil

For the Sauce:

- 6 fresh sage leaves
- 2 tablespoons (30 g) unsalted butter
- 1 shallot, diced
- 2 ounces (56 g) dried porcini mushrooms, or 1 cup chopped fresh wild mushrooms
- 1-1/2 cups (350 ml) heavy cream
- 3 tablespoons (45 ml) brandy
- Grated Parmesan, for garnish
- Chopped fresh parsley, for garnish

Instructions:

To make the filling, melt the butter in a sauté pan, add the squash, and cook until soft, about 15 minutes. If the squash gets too watery, cook for a little longer. Transfer the squash to a plate and smash it using a fork, potato ricer, or potato masher; allow the squash to cool. Stir in the Parmesan and nutmeg, then season with salt and white pepper to taste. The filling must be firm, sticking to a spoon even if turned upside down. Reserve in the refrigerator until ready to use.

To make the dough, place the flour in a large bowl. Make a well in the center of the flour and add the salt, beaten eggs, and oil. Using your hands or a plastic spatula, mix until well combined. Transfer the dough to a lightly floured surface and knead until elastic and smooth, about 10 minutes. If necessary, add more flour to prevent the dough from sticking. Cover with plastic wrap and let rest for at least 30 minutes.

To make the sauce, tear the sage by hand into small pieces. In a sauté pan over medium heat, melt the butter and sauté the shallots, sage, and mushrooms until the shallots are soft and translucent. Add the cream and turn the heat to low. Add the brandy and cook the sauce gently until it reduces slightly. Remove from heat and set aside.

To assemble and cook the raviolis, bring a large stockpot of salted water to a boil. Divide the pasta dough into quarters. Using a pasta machine, form sheets of pasta 1/16 inch (1.5 mm) thick. Cut the sheets into 4 x 4-inch (10 x 10-cm) squares. Place a dollop of filling in the middle of each pasta square and fold to form a triangle. Press the edges together gently to avoid air gaps, and seal the edges of the ravioli with your fingers. If the pasta is not sticking together well, use a small pastry brush to moisten the edges with water before resealing. Repeat the process to form more raviolis until you've used up the pasta and filling.

Add the raviolis to the pot of boiling water, reduce the heat to a simmer, and cook for about 3 minutes, until they start floating to the top and the pasta is al dente. Drain the raviolis and place them on a warmed serving platter. Cover with the sauce and sprinkle with Parmesan and parsley.

You can make extra raviolis and freeze them for later use. They will last in the freezer for about 3 months.

Bucatini with Quail Sauce

Since partridges are difficult to find nowadays, quail is substituted in this delicious dish.

Serves 6 to 8

Ingredient

- 6 quails, halved
- Salt and freshly ground white pepper
- 4 tablespoons (1/2 stick/60 g) unsalted butter
- 2 tablespoons (30 ml) olive oil
- 6 cloves garlic, chopped
- 1 sprig sage
- 1 tablespoon all-purpose flour
- 1/2 cup (120 ml) good-quality red wine (such as Merlot or Cabernet Sauvignon)
- 6 white mushrooms, finely chopped
- 1 small yellow onion, finely diced
- 1 (14 oz/400 g) can Italian crushed tomatoes
- 1 cup (240 ml) chicken stock or beef stock
- 1 lb. (450 g) bucatini pasta (if necessary, substitute with spaghetti)
- Grated Parmesan, for garnish

Instructions:

Pat the quail pieces dry with a paper towel, then season them generously with salt and white pepper. Melt the butter with the olive oil in a heavy-bottomed pan over medium to high heat. When the butter is almost smoking, arrange the quail in the pan so that the pieces do not overlap; depending on the size of your pan, you may need to cook the quail in batches. Cook for 3 to 4 minutes, turning occasionally, until the skin is golden; don't worry about undercooking, as the quails will finish cooking in the sauce. Remove the quails from the pan and set aside to rest. Add the chopped garlic and sage to the leftover juices in the frying pan. Once the garlic turns golden, add the onion and sprinkle the flour over the mixture. Stir for 1 minute, then add the wine, mushrooms, tomatoes, and stock. When the liquid comes to a low boil, return the quail to the pan. Reduce the heat to the lowest setting possible, cover the pan, and let the quail simmer gently in the sauce for about 1 hour. Scrape the bottom of the pan every 20 minutes or so and add water if the sauce becomes too thick.

While the quail sauce is simmering, bring a large pot of water to boil and cook the bucatini according to the package directions. Drain the pasta well and transfer to a serving platter. Pour the quail sauce over the pasta and garnish with Parmesan.

Lemony basil orzo pasta salad

A fantastic summer treat, this recipe offers great texture and flavors. It is perfect for a bento lunch box!

Makes: 10

Time: 9 minutes

Ingredient

- 1 lb. Orzo pasta, 1 pound
- 4 tbsp. Salt
- ½ cup chopped roasted red peppers
- Lemon zest of 2 large lemons
- 1 bunch chopped fresh basil,
- ½ cup olive oil
- ½ cup chopped fresh flat leaf parsley
- 2 cups yellow and red grape tomatoes, diced
- ½ cup green onions
- ½ cup lemon juice

Directions

Add the salt to boiling water and cook off 9 minutes. Drain and set.

As the pasta is being cooked, prepare a dressing – mix together lemon juice, zest and olive oil.

Add in the pasta and veggies. Toss well.

Refrigerate overnight or for 2 hours before packing into your bento box.

Spaghetti with Meatballs

This recipe makes a delicious spaghetti dish perfect for a date night dinner!

Serving Size: 4 servings

Total Time: 1hr

Ingredient

Meatballs

- 1 pounds ground pork sausage
- 1 pounds ground beef
- 2 cloves crushed garlic
- 2 tbsp. fresh basil, chopped
- ¾ cup grated parmesan
- 2 tbsp. fresh chives, chopped
- ½ tsp. black pepper powder
- ½ tsp. pepper flakes
- ¼ cup milk
- 1 tsp. salt
- 2 eggs
- ½ packet crackers, finely crushed

Raw Marinara Sauce

- 1 can diced tomatoes
- ¼ cup fresh basil leaves
- 1 sprig fresh oregano leaves
- 1 garlic clove
- 5 oil packed sun dried tomato halves
- 1 tbsp. lemon juice
- 2 tbsp. olive oil
- ¼ tsp. salt
- Pinch of pepper

Pasta

- 1 pound spaghetti

Instructions:

Meatballs: Preheat oven to 400 degrees. Combine all meatball ingredients in a large ball and mix by hand until just combined.

Divide and roll into golf sized balls.

Place on a greased, foil-lined baking sheet.

Bake the meatballs for 20 minutes.

Sauce: Combine all sauce ingredients in a blender and blend till smooth.

Pour into a large saucepan and bring to a simmer. Carefully add in the meatballs and continue to simmer for an extra 10 minutes. Stir gently.

Pasta: In a large pot, bring 4 quarts of water to a boil. Sprinkle in salt. Add the spaghetti and cook until done – 8 to 10 minutes.

To serve: Layer spaghetti in a serving dish and top with meatball mixture. Sprinkle with Parmesan cheese and enjoy!

Mexican Mac and Cheese

Classic mac and cheese takes a south-of-the-border turn with the addition of a chipotle in adobo, which gives a hint of heat, and the crushed tortillas and Cotija cheese are used for the topping.

Makes: 6 servings

Prep: 10 mins

Cook: 40 mins

Ingredient

- Salt
- 8 ounces uncooked wagon wheel macaroni
- 2 Tablespoons unsalted butter
- ½ tablespoon minced garlic
- 2 Tablespoons all-purpose flour
- 1 teaspoon ground cumin
- ¾ cup finely chopped onion
- 2 cups milk
- 1 chipotle en adobo, chopped
- ½ teaspoon ground coriander
- ½ cup sundried tomatoes, thinly sliced
- 2 ¼ cups grated sharp Cheddar cheese
- 1 cup grated Jack cheese
- 1 ½ cups crushed tortilla chips
- 1 1/3 cups freshly grated Cotija cheese

Directions

Cook the pasta according to package directions. Remove, drain, and set aside.

Heat a 10-inch cast-iron skillet over med. heat until hot. Add the butter, onion, garlic, cumin, and coriander, and cook over medium-low heat, stirring often, until the onion is softened, about 7 minutes.

Preheat your oven to 350°F.

Add the flour to the softened onions and stir continuously for 3 minutes. Whisk in the milk and bring to a boil. Reduce & simmer for 2 minutes. Add the chipotle and tomatoes and cool slightly; add the cheeses and stir until melted. Stir the pasta into the cheese mixture.

In a bowl, toss the tortilla chips and Cotija cheese together and drizzle on top of the macaroni. Bake until the dish is hot and the top is golden brown, 25 to 30 minutes. Serve.

Pasta Pizza Chicken Casserole

Pasta, pizza, and shredded chicken casserole with onions and bell peppers.

Makes: 4-6 servings

Prep: 5 mins

Cook: 25 mins

Ingredient

- 4 cups cooked small shell pasta
- 2 cups shredded cooked chicken
- 1 jar (16 ounces) pizza sauce
- 1 small onion, sliced
- ½ green bell pepper, sliced

Directions

Preheat oven to 350 degrees.

Mix all the ingredients in a greased 9x13-inch casserole dish. Cover and bake for 25 mins. or until heated through.

Serve.

Arrabiata Sauce

This hearty sauce is both delicious and easy to make! Layer overcooked pasta to make an entire meal out of it.

Total Time: 35m

Makes: 6 servings

Ingredient

- 1 tsp. olive oil
- 1 cup onion, finely chopped
- 4 cloves garlic, minced
- 7 tbsp. red wine
- 1 tbsp. white sugar
- 1 tbsp. fresh basil, roughly chopped
- 1 tsp. red pepper flakes
- 2 tbsp. tomato paste
- 1 tbsp. lemon juice
- ½ tsp. Italian seasoning
- ¼ tsp. black pepper
- 2, 14.5 ounce cans of tomatoes, peeled and finely diced
- 2 tbsp. of parsley, roughly chopped

Instructions:

First heat up some oil in a large sized skillet placed over medium heat. Once the oil is hot enough add in the garlic and onions and cook for at least five minutes.

Then add in the wine, white sugar, fresh basil, peppers, tomato paste, fresh lemon juice, Italian seasoning, tomatoes and a dash of pepper. Stir thoroughly to combine and bring to a boil.

Reduce the heat to low and allow to simmer for the next 15 minutes.

After this time add in the fresh parsley and remove from heat. Serve over a bed of pasta and enjoy.

Cheese and Salsa Chicken Casserole

Pasta and Chicken Casserole with Salsa and Cheese.

Makes: 4-6 Servings

Prep: 5 mins

Cook: 25 mins

Ingredient

- 4 cups cooked small shell pasta
- 2 cups chopped cooked chicken
- 1 jar (16 ounces) medium salsa
- 2 cups grated Mexican-blend cheese

Directions

Preheat oven to 350 degrees.

Combine all ingredients in a greased 9x13-inch casserole dish. Cover and bake 20–25 mins. or until heated through.

Serve.

Lasagna

A delicious, classic lasagna recipe.

Makes: 8 servings

Prep: 25 mins

Cook: 1 ½ hrs.

Ingredient

- Unsalted butter, for the dish
- 1 recipe (4 cups) Thick Béchamel
- ½ recipe (6 sheets; about 8 ounces) Fresh Pasta Sheet
- ½ recipe (3 cups) Ragu Bolognese, warm
- 4 oz. freshly grated Parmesan cheese

Directions

Preheat oven to 375F.

Assemble the lasagna: Mix together ½ cup of the béchamel sauce and ¼ cup of room-temperature water and put in a 9 by 13inch (3-quart) glass or ceramic baking dish, then top with one third of the noodles (2 sheets). Put 1 cup of the béchamel sauce on the pasta and cover with 1½ cups of the Bolognese sauce. Sprinkle with ⅓ cup of the Parmesan. Repeat with another layer of noodles, 1 cup of the béchamel, the remaining Bolognese sauce, and ⅓ cup of the Parmesan. Top with the remaining noodles, béchamel, and Parmesan.

Bake the lasagna: Cover with foil and bake for 30 mins. Uncover & bake until bubbling and the top is golden, about 20 minutes longer. Let rest for 15 minutes before cutting into squares and serving.

Linguine with Tuna Puttanesca

Create an Italian-inspired dish that is fit for a feast in under half an hour by tossing together these simple ingredients. This dish has a colorful past, it is famously named after Italy's 'ladies of the night' who, it is said very quickly made it in between clients!

Portions: 4

Total Time: 27mins

Ingredient

- Salt
- 12 ounces linguine
- 2 tbsp. extra virgin olive oil
- 4 cloves of garlic (thinly sliced)
- ½ tsp red pepper flakes
- 2 tbsp. capers (drained)
- ½ cup Kalamata olives (roughly chopped)
- 1 (28 ounce) can Italian plum tomatoes
- 4 basil leaves (torn)
- 1 (5 ounce) can albacore tuna in olive oil
- Ground black pepper
- Basil leaves (to garnish)

Directions:

Fill a large pan with salt and water and bring to boil. Then add the linguine and cook until the linguine is al dente.

In the meantime, over moderate heat, heat the olive oil in large frying pan or skillet.

Add the sliced garlic along with the red pepper flakes then while stirring, cook until just toasted, this will take around 1-2 minutes.

Next, add the drained capers and Kalamata olives and sauté for another 2 minutes.

Put the tomatoes in a bowl, and using clean hands, pick up and crush the plum tomatoes into the pan, setting aside the juices.

Cook until the crushed tomatoes are a just dry, for 2-3 minutes. Add the juices reserved earlier, along with the torn basil and a pinch of kosher salt to season and cook until the sauce begins to thicken, 2 minutes.

Add the tuna together with the olive oil and using a metal fork break it up. Season again with a pinch of salt.

Drain the linguine, reserving ½ cup of the pasta water, and returning the linguine to the pot. Add the sauce and the reserved water and toss.

Season and garnish with basil.

Spicy Pasta Alfredo Casserole

Classic Alfredo made spicy thanks to the roasted red peppers and chilies.

Makes: 6 servings

Prep: 10 mins

Cook: 1 hr.

Ingredient

- 1 (12 oz.) package fettuccini
- 1/2 cup butter
- 2 cups heavy cream
- 1/2 cup water
- 2 clove garlic, crushed
- 3 cups grated Parmesan cheese
- 1/2 cup fresh parsley, chopped
- 1 (16 oz.) carton sour cream
- 1 can diced tomatoes & green chiles, drained
- 1 (14 oz.) jar artichoke hearts, drained, quartered
- 1 jar roasted red peppers, first drained, & chopped

Directions

Cook fettuccini according to package instructions; drain well and set aside.

In a med saucepan, melt the butter on med heat. Stir in heavy cream and water; simmer for 5 minutes. Mix in garlic and 2 cups cheese; whisk quickly, heating through. Remove from heat and stir in parsley. Stir in sour cream and tomatoes with green chiles.

Combine pasta, sauce, artichoke hearts and red peppers. Spoon into a greased 9x13x2-inch baking dish. Cover & bake at 350F. for 45 minutes. Add last cup of cheese on top; bake for 10 minutes more.

Tortellini Chicken Primavera

Chicken, pasta, and pesto sauce make up this scrumptious recipe.

Makes: 6 servings

Prep: 10 mins

Cook: 15 mins

Ingredient

- 1 1/2 to 2 lbs. boneless, skinless chicken breast meat, cubed
- 2 to 3 cloves garlic, minced
- 1/2 tablespoon dried basil
- 1 1/2 cups water
- 3 cups tortellini
- 1 container pesto sauce
- 3 to 4 Roma tomatoes, chopped
- 1 red bell pepper, chopped
- 1 yellow bell pepper, chopped
- 1 zucchini, sliced
- Parmesan cheese, shredded, for garnish

Directions

In a Dutch oven, stew chicken, garlic and basil with water. Cook over med high heat till all the water evaporates. In a separate pan, cook pasta as directed on package until al dente; drain. In a large serving dish, toss pasta, chicken and pesto sauce with bell peppers and zucchini. Sprinkle with Parmesan cheese. Serve.

Conclusion

There you go! Delicious pasta recipes for you to make at home! Make dinner (or lunch!) fun with these delicious recipes! From creamy and cheesy to spicy and sour, there's a variety of recipes to try out! Enjoy!

About the Author

A native of Indianapolis, Indiana, Valeria Ray found her passion for cooking while she was studying English Literature at Oakland City University. She decided to try a cooking course with her friends and the experience changed her forever. She enrolled at the Art Institute of Indiana which offered extensive courses in the culinary Arts. Once Ray dipped her toe in the cooking world, she never looked back.

When Valeria graduated, she worked in French restaurants in the Indianapolis area until she became the head chef at one of the 5-star establishments in the area. Valeria's attention to taste and visual detail caught the eye of a local business person who expressed an interest in publishing her recipes. Valeria began her secondary career authoring cookbooks and e-books which she tackled with as much talent and gusto as her first career. Her passion for food leaps off the page of her books which have colourful anecdotes and stunning pictures of dishes she has prepared herself.

Valeria Ray lives in Indianapolis with her husband of 15 years, Tom, her daughter, Isobel and their loveable Golden Retriever, Goldy. Valeria enjoys cooking special dishes in her large, comfortable kitchen where the family gets involved in preparing meals. This successful, dynamic chef is an inspiration to culinary students and novice cooks everywhere.

Author's Afterthoughts

Thank you for Purchasing my book and taking the time to read it from front to back. I am always grateful when a reader chooses my work and I hope you enjoyed it!

With the vast selection available online, I am touched that you chose to be purchasing my work and take valuable time out of your life to read it. My hope is that you feel you made the right decision.

I very much would like to know what you thought of the book. Please take the time to write an honest and informative review on Amazon.com. Your experience and opinions will be of great benefit to me and those readers looking to make an informed choice.

With much thanks,

Valeria Ray

Printed in Great Britain
by Amazon